ASTROLOGY
SELF-CARE

Aquarius

ASTROLOGY
SELF-CARE

Aquarius

Live your best life
by the stars

Sarah Bartlett

First published in Great Britain in 2022 by Yellow Kite
An imprint of Hodder & Stoughton
An Hachette UK company

1

A CIP catalogue record for this title is available
from the British Library

Illustrations © shutterstock.com

Hardback ISBN 978 1 399 70488 5
eBook ISBN 978 1 399 70490 8
Audiobook ISBN 978 1 399 70489 2

Typeset in Nocturne Serif by Hewer Text UK Ltd, Edinburgh

Designed by Goldust Design

Printed and bound in Great Britain by Clays Ltd, Elcograf S.p.A.

Hodder & Stoughton policy is to use papers that
are natural, renewable and recyclable products and made
from wood grown in sustainable forests. The logging and
manufacturing processes are expected to conform to
the environmental regulations of the country of origin.

Yellow Kite
Hodder & Stoughton Ltd
Carmelite House
50 Victoria Embankment
London EC4Y 0DZ

www.yellowkitebooks.co.uk

I am not eccentric. It's just that I am more alive than most people. I am an unpopular electric eel set in a pond of catfish.

Edith Sitwell (1887–1964)

There is a path, hidden between the road of reason and the hedgerow of dreams, which leads to the secret garden of self-knowledge. This book will show you the way.

Contents

Introduction

The ancient Greek goddess Gaia arose from Chaos and was the personification of the Earth and all of Nature. One of the first primordial beings, along with Tartarus (the Underworld), Eros (love) and Nyx (night), as mother of all life, she is both the embodiment of all that this planet is and its spiritual caretaker.

It's hardly likely you will want to become a full-time Mother Earth, but many of us right now are caring more about our beautiful planet and all that lives upon it. To nurture and respect this amazing place we call home, and to preserve this tiny dot in the Universe, the best place to start is, well, with you.

Self-care is about respecting and honouring who you are as an individual. It's about realising that nurturing yourself is neither vanity nor a conceit, but a creative act that brings an awesome sense of awareness and a deeper connection to the Universe and all that's in it. Caring about yourself means you care about everything in the cosmos – because you are part of it.

But self-care isn't just about trekking to the gym, jogging around the park or eating the right foods. It's also about discovering who you are becoming as an individual and caring for that authenticity (and loving and caring about who we are becoming means others can love and care about us, too). This is where the art of sun-sign astrology comes in.

Astrology And Self-Care

So what is astrology? And how can it direct each of us to the right self-care pathway? Put simply, astrology is the study of the planets, sun and moon and their influence on events and people here on Earth. It is an art that has been used for thousands of years to forecast world events, military and political outcomes and, more recently, financial market trends. As such, it is an invaluable tool for understanding our own individuality and how to be true to ourselves. Although there is still dispute within astrological circles as to whether the planets actually physically affect us, there is strong evidence to show that the cycles and patterns they create in the sky have a direct mirroring effect on what happens down here on Earth and, more importantly, on each individual's personality.

Your horoscope or birth-chart is a snapshot of the planets, sun and moon in the sky at the moment you were born. This amazing picture reveals all your innate potential, characteristics and qualities. In fact, it is probably the best 'selfie' you could ever have! Astrology can not only tell you who you are, but also how best to care for that self and your own specific needs and desires as revealed by your birth-chart.

Self-care is simply time to look after yourself – to

restore, inspirit and refresh and love your unique self. But it's also about understanding, accepting and being aware of your own traits – both the good and not so good – so that you can then say, 'It's ok to be me, and my intention is to become the best of myself'. In fact, by looking up to the stars and seeing how they reflect us down here on Earth, we can deepen our connection to the Universe for the good of all, too. Understanding that caring about ourselves is not selfish creates an awesome sense of self-acceptance and awareness.

So how does each of us honour the individual 'me' and find the right kind of rituals and practices to suit our personalities? Astrology sorts us out into the zodiac – an imaginary belt encircling the Earth divided into twelve sun signs; so, for example, what one sign finds relaxing, another may find a hassle or stressful. When it comes to physical fitness, adventurous Arians thrive on aerobic work, while soulful Pisceans feel nurtured by yoga. Financial reward or status would inspire the ambitious Capricorn mind, while theatrical Leos need to indulge their joy of being centre stage.

By knowing which sun sign you are and its associated characteristics, you will discover the right self-care routines and practices to suit you. And this unique and empowering book is here to help – with all the rituals and practices in these pages specifically suited to your sun-sign personality for nurturing and vitalising your mind, body and spirit.

However, self-care is not an excuse to be lazy and avoid the goings on in the rest of the world. Self-care is about taking responsibility for our choices and understanding our unique essence, so that we can engage with all aspects of ourselves and the way we interact with the world.

IN A NUTSHELL

Aquarius loves being innovative, discovering ideas and challenging the status quo. In fact, if Aquarians don't have a mission to radically revise something that's tried and trusted, they become bored or frustrated. This book will not only boost inspired thinking, but guide you to fulfil your dreams, invent new ways to help others and, most of all, to discover how to get in touch with your greatest gift – and that's to make a lasting impression on the world.

Sun-Sign Astrology

Also known as your star sign or zodiac sign, your sun sign encompasses the following:

* Your solar identity, or sense of self
* What really matters to you
* Your future intentions
* Your sense of purpose
* Various qualities that manifest through your actions, goals, desires and the personal sense of being 'you'
* Your sense of being 'centred' – whether 'self-centred' (too much ego) or 'self-conscious' (too little ego); in other words, how you perceive who you are as an individual

In fact, the sun tells you how you can 'shine' best to become who you really are.

ASTROLOGY FACTS

The zodiac or sun signs are twelve 30-degree segments that create an imaginary belt around the Earth. The zodiac belt is also known as the ecliptic, which is the apparent path of the sun as it travels round the Earth during the year.

The sun or zodiac signs are further divided into four elements (Fire, Earth, Air and Water, denoting a certain energy ruling each sign), plus three modalities (qualities associated with how we interact with the world; these are known as Cardinal, Fixed and Mutable). So as an Aquarian, for example, you are a 'Fixed Air' sign.

* Fire signs: Aries, Leo, Sagittarius
  They are: extrovert, passionate, assertive

* Earth signs: Taurus, Virgo, Capricorn
  They are: practical, materialistic, sensual

* Air signs: Gemini, Libra, Aquarius
* They are: communicative, innovative, inquisitive

* Water signs: Cancer, Scorpio, Pisces
  They are: emotional, intuitive, understanding

The modalities are based on their seasonal resonance according to the northern hemisphere.

Cardinal signs instigate and initiate ideas and projects.
They are: Aries, Cancer, Libra and Capricorn

Fixed signs resolutely build and shape ideas.
They are: Taurus, Leo, Scorpio and Aquarius

Mutable signs generate creative change and adapt ideas to reach a conclusion.

They are: Gemini, Virgo, Sagittarius and Pisces

Planetary rulers

Each zodiac sign is assigned a planet, which highlights the qualities of that sign:

Aries is ruled by Mars (fearless)
Taurus is ruled by Venus (indulgent)
Gemini is ruled by Mercury (magical)
Cancer is ruled by the moon (instinctive)
Leo is ruled by the sun (empowering)
Virgo is ruled by Mercury (informative)
Libra is ruled by Venus (compassionate)
Scorpio is ruled by Pluto (passionate)
Sagittarius is ruled by Jupiter (adventurous)
Capricorn is ruled by Saturn (disciplined)
Aquarius is ruled by Uranus (innovative)
Pisces is ruled by Neptune (imaginative)

Opposite Signs

Signs oppose one another across the zodiac (i.e. those that are 180 degrees away from each other) – for example, Aquarius opposes Leo and Taurus opposes Scorpio. We often find ourselves mysteriously attracted to our opposite signs in romantic relationships, and while the signs' traits appear to clash in this 'polarity', the essence of each is contained in the other (note, they have the same modality). Gaining insight into the characteristics of your opposite sign (which are, essentially, inherent in you) can deepen your understanding of the energetic interplay of the horoscope.

On The Cusp

Some of us are born 'on the cusp' of two signs – in other words, the day or time when the sun moved from one zodiac sign to another. If you were born at the end or beginning of the dates usually given in horoscope pages (the sun's move through one sign usually lasts approximately four weeks), you can check which sign you are by contacting a reputable astrologer (or astrology site) (see Resources, p. 115) who will calculate it exactly for you. For example, 23 August is the standardised changeover day for the sun to move into Virgo and out of Leo. But every year, the time and even sometimes the day the sun changes sign can differ. So, say you were born on 23 August at five in the morning and the sun didn't move into Virgo until five in the afternoon on that day, you would be a Leo, not a Virgo.

How To Use This Book

The book is divided into three parts, each guiding you in applying self-care to different areas of your life:

* Part One: your mind and feelings
* Part Two: your body
* Part Three: your soul

Caring about the mind using rituals or ideas tailored to your sign shows you ways to unlock stress, restore focus or widen your perception. Applying the practices in Part One will connect you to your feelings and help you to acknowledge and become aware of why your emotions are as they are and how to deal with them. This sort of emotional self-care will set you up to deal with your relationships better, enhance all forms of communication and ensure you know exactly how to ask for what you want or need, and be true to your deepest desires.

A WORD ON CHAKRAS

Eastern spiritual traditions maintain that universal energy, known as 'prana' in India and 'chi' in Chinese philosophy, flows through the body, linked by seven subtle energy centres known as chakras (Sanskrit for 'wheel'). These energies are believed to revolve or spiral around and through our bodies, vibrating at different frequencies (corresponding to seven colours of the light spectrum) in an upward, vertical direction. Specific crystals are placed on the chakras to heal, harmonise, stimulate or subdue the chakras if imbalance is found.

The seven chakras are:
* The base or root (found at the base of the spine)
* The sacral (mid-belly)
* The solar plexus (between belly and chest)
* The heart (centre of chest)
* The throat (throat)
* The third eye (between the eyebrows)
* The crown (top of the head)

On p. 91 we will look in more detail at how Aquarians can work with chakras for self-care.

Fitness and caring for the body are different for all of us, too. While Aquarius benefits from hiking, for example, Taurus thrives on aromatherapy sessions and Gemini a quick daily stretch or yoga. Delve into Part Two whenever you're in need of physical restoration or a sensual makeover tailored to your sign.

Spiritual self-care opens you to your sacred self or soul. Which is why Part Three looks at how you can nurture your soul according to your astrological sun sign. It shows you how to connect to and care for your spirituality in simple ways, such as being at one with Nature or just enjoying the world around you. It will show you how to be more positive about who you are and honour your connection to the Universe. In fact, all the rituals and practices in this section will bring you joyful relating, harmonious living and a true sense of happiness.

The Key

Remember, your birth-chart or horoscope is like the key to a treasure chest containing the most precious jewels that make you you. Learn about them, and care for them well. Use this book to polish, nurture, respect and give value to the beautiful gemstones of who you are, and, in doing so, bring your potential to life. It's your right to be true to who you are, just by virtue of being born on this planet, and therefore being a child of Mother Earth and the cosmos.

Care for you, and you care for the Universe.

AQUARIUS
WORDS OF WISDOM

As you embark on your self-care journey, it's important to look at the lunar cycles and specific astrological moments throughout the year. At those times (and, indeed, at any time you choose), the words of Aquarius wisdom below will be invaluable, empowering you with positive energy. Taking a few mindful moments at each of the four major phases of every lunar cycle and at the two important astrological moments in your solar year (see Glossary, p. 117) will affirm and enhance your positive attitude towards caring about yourself and the world.

NEW CRESCENT MOON – to care for yourself:

'I won't be diverted from my purpose, nor will I try to divert others from theirs.'

'I will only expect the unexpected.'
'There is always a way to achieve success, if I draw on intuition as well as logic.'

FULL MOON – for sealing your intention to care for your feeling world:

'Through creative self-expression I give value to my emotions.'

'Rather than curse in the darkness, it is timely to light a candle.'

'If I accept that I have feelings, I will understand my place in the Universe.'

WANING MOON – for letting go, and letting things be:

'If I want the world to be a better place, I must give up the idea that I can't change myself.'

'I must learn to accept that other people's opinions may be different from my own.'

'I will make my own choices, then I will only have myself to blame, and no one else.'

DARK OF THE MOON – to acknowledge your 'shadow' side:

'When I feel strongly about something, I must express it clearly.'

'I am often awkward for the sake of being so.'

'I accept I am eclectic, electrifying and eccentric, and must learn to let other people be who they are, too.'

SOLAR RETURN SALUTATION – welcoming your new solar year to be true to who you are:

Repeat on your birthday: 'I can help make a difference to the world because I am a citizen of the world.'

SUN IN OPPOSITION – learn to be open to the opposite perspective that lies within you:

Repeat when the sun is in Leo: 'My opposite sign is Leo – a sign of ego, self-importance, dramatic expression and fiery exuberance. These attributes are part of my birth-chart, too, so I go to meet them with an open mind. I will care for the lion within and remember that "innovation is for the world" and "I did it my way".'

The Aquarius Personality

~~~

*It's the possibility of having a dream
come true that makes life interesting.*
Paulo Coelho, *The Alchemist*

Characteristics: Quirky, aloof, avant-garde,
independent, intellectual, glamorous, idealistic,
altruistic, eccentric, contrary, rebellious, inventive,
humanitarian, experimental, shocking, solitary,
non-conformist, self-controlled, opinionated,
unemotional, stubborn

Symbol: the Water Bearer
A mythical cup bearer pours the 'waters of life' into
the world; Aquarius, similarly, is a cosmic caregiver,
offering humanity the power of innovation, radical
thought, progress and knowledge.

Planetary ruler: Uranus (and traditionally Saturn)
Uranus is an ice giant, a gassy wilderness, where

winds blow up to 560 miles per hour. The strange tilt of Uranus means that one pole or the other is usually pointed towards the sun. Standing on the north pole of Uranus, you would see the sun rise in the sky and circle around for forty-two years. By the end of this amazing 'summer', the sun would finally disappear below the horizon. This would be followed by forty-two years of darkness or Uranian 'winter'.

Astrological Uranus (and traditionally Saturn) in the birth-chart: Uranus represents rebellion, ideology and non-conformity; Saturn represents limitation, rules and convention. Put the two together and you have the complex nature of Aquarius – a civilised rebel with a cause.

Element: Air
Air signs delight in all forms of communication and knowledge. They are intellectual, curious and have analytical minds. Their feeling world is uncomfortable and they prefer to live with their heads in the clouds, rather than in the messy waters of emotions.

Modality: Fixed
Fixed signs follow the rules, as long as they're rules they've set for themselves. Aquarians use this somewhat inflexible approach to life to help them plan and project into the future, underscoring a

determination to succeed. They avoid those who want to change them or anything that puts them off their course.

Body: In astrology, each sign rules various parts of the body. Aquarius traditionally rules the ankles, lower legs and peripheral circulatory system.

Crystal: Amber

Sun-sign profile: Individualists, admired for their eccentric and sometimes perverse outlook on life, Aquarians feel they bear the weight of humanity, Nature and the planet on their shoulders, often sacrificing their own personal needs in the process. The Water Bearer can be shocking, awkward for the sake of being awkward and contrary just when they choose to be. Like the other Air signs, they prefer a logical, analytical lifestyle, rather than a feeling, subjective one. Aquarians' potential for making a mark on the world is enormous. This may manifest through art, science, politics or just caring for the garden, but whichever pathway they choose, living out their potential for changing things (apart from themselves) brings them the happiness they seek.

Your best-kept secret: Few people realise that it's often what you *don't do* that sets you apart from the crowd. For example, you decide not to wear socks, you don't do things by the book, you don't do social media when other people expect you to, you don't have the same style of home as everyone else . . . Put simply, you don't conform.

What gives you meaning and purpose in life? An Aquarian's raison d'être is a consuming passion for changing the world for the better – for being the ultimate cosmic caregiver, overturning traditional systems and discovering universal truths. You intuitively tap into future trends and follow your nose to inspire your creative genius.

What makes you feel good to be you? Personal freedom, intelligent thinking, a minimalist, off-grid, green or alternative lifestyle, unusual ideas, equality, being unselfish, reforming others, surprises, your own opinions, travel

What or who do you identify with? Reformers, people who have made their mark on the world either by improving its welfare or creating beneficial radical change, such as rebels, visionaries, renegades, innovators, original thinkers, artists, geniuses

What stresses you out? Emotion, weepy friends, possessiveness, bigotry, human weakness, lack of discipline, changes you didn't make, people who get too physically close, being given orders

What relaxes you? Fresh air, outdoor activities, good books, painting, art, walking, being alone for a while, finding a cause, helping a charity, friends who don't expect anything from you, planning how to change the world

What challenges you? Emotional scenes, intimate relationships, people who think they know better than you, conventional rules and expectations

What Does Self-Care Mean For Aquarius?

Aquarians can't stand being slotted into any fitness, spiritual or dietary category. They're so single-minded about their image, body shape, beliefs and insights, they rarely follow anyone else's ideas if they can help it. If anyone says to them, 'You should try this out' or, 'You should take more care of yourself', that's the trigger for them to instantly rebel and to care less than ever. In fact, the words 'should' and 'care' are often absent from the Aquarian vocabulary. They may well know what's best for the rest of the world, but no one else knows what's best for them.

Aquarians are ahead of their time and know all about the latest self-care fads before anyone else. On the other hand, when it comes to actually practising self-care on a regular basis, they can take it or leave it. Being constrained by specific routines, practices or fitness goals prompts the Aquarian perversity of doing exactly the opposite: namely, doing none of it! But if they are to make their dreams come true or make a lasting impression in changing the world for the better, they need to look after themselves a bit, too.

Self-Care Focus

The good news is this book isn't about personal grooming and it isn't going to try to change you. What it will do is reveal your incredible talent, promoting a greater sense of self-understanding and of your place in this big, wide world. It will inspire you, maximising and enhancing your strengths, so you can become the cosmic caregiver you yearn to be, so fulfilling your astrological potential.

In fact, caring for your body, mind and spirit isn't such a selfish thing, after all.

So let's try replacing the words 'self-care' with 'self-understanding' – because if you acquire more understanding about your unique personality, that might just be of benefit to the planet. Give it a try, and perhaps surprise yourself a little.

PART ONE

Caring For Your Mind And Feelings

Two roads diverged in a wood, and I—
I took the one less traveled by,
And that has made all the difference.

Robert Frost, 'The Road Not Taken'

This section will inspire you to delight in your thoughts, express your ideas and take pleasure in your feelings. Once you get that deep sense of awareness of who you are and what you need, not only will it feel good to be alive, but you will be even more content to be yourself. The rituals and practices here will boost your self-esteem, motivate you to lead a more serene existence and enhance all forms of relationships with others. The most important relationship of all, with yourself, will be nurtured in the best possible way according to your sun sign.

What a penetrating mind you have. Searching, observing, experimental and insightful. When those moments of illumination come to you, they're like flashes of divine lightning or chariots of fire. However, the Aquarius mind is a double-edged sword: at once wondrous in its power to analyse – and by golly, do you analyse – and self-sabotaging in its attempts to keep all feelings under control.

No one is really sure if 'thought' generates feeling or 'feeling' creates thought. Some schools proclaim both are caused by genetics or something chemical going on in our bodies (hormones). But whatever the root of feelings and thoughts, we all have these 'things' and we have to work out how to accept and integrate them. The problem is, Aquarians don't always have patience for human feeling (it gets in the way of all those abstract ideas), and rarely have time to contemplate their own emotional worlds.

The practices below will allow you to begin to understand the positive aspects of both mind and feelings, and care about them more.

A DAILY MANTRA

There are no daily fixed routines (hurrah!) – however, you could repeat this simple affirmation every day, perhaps when you're walking, working, sleeping, eating breakfast:

'If I want to make a difference to the planet, I must first make a difference to myself.'

THE WATER-BEARER RITUAL

The great god Zeus, seducer of mortals, nymphs and assorted gods and goddesses, swept down to Earth and chose the mortal youth Ganymede to be his cup bearer in Olympus (apparently dishing out wine and nectar at all those heavenly parties). He later placed Ganymede in the sky as the Water-Bearer constellation.

The sign of Aquarius is often erroneously associated with the element of Water because of the Water-Bearer symbol. But, of course, Aquarius is an Air sign, and has nothing to do with the feeling world of the actual Water signs (Cancer, Scorpio and Pisces). So Ganymede's message is, in fact, 'I offer the feelings of life to humanity, but it's for the world to experience and understand these emotions'.

Here's a ritual to get in touch with those feelings that you are sharing out to the world.

You will need:
* A large bowl of water
* 4 crystals – a clear quartz to represent Air, a red one to represent Fire, a green one to represent Earth and a blue one to represent Water

1. Sit before your bowl and place the crystals gently into the water one by one, in the order of Air, Earth, Fire, Water. As you do so, say one line for each crystal:

'This is my Air, my breath, my thoughts.'
'This is my Earth, my roots, my senses.'
'This is my Fire, my desire, my goals.'
'This is my Water, my feelings, my soul.'

2. Reflect for a moment upon the crystals in the water and imagine they are all symbolic of your own qualities. There, in the water, you will find passion, thoughts, feelings of anger but also of love, of goodness and of acceptance of self.

3. Plunge your hands in gently and hold each crystal in turn, for a little while. When you touch the blue crystal, imagine you are connecting to your feeling world, and how that can actually feel good, too.

URANIAN ENERGY PRACTICE

Your ruling planet is Uranus. The cyan blue of its atmosphere is caused by methane, and the tilt of the planet's axis is so bizarre that it rotates from east to west (only Venus and Uranus do this) and on its side. Some authorities believe Uranus has liquid diamond at its core, and it also has an unusual magnetic field due to its strange rotation, creating millions of miles of corkscrew-like waves trailing through space.

To nurture and embrace your cool Uranian energy, the freezing winds of your amazing mind, the erratic energy you release into the atmosphere and your diamond core, please enjoy this visualisation practice:

1. Stand outside in the fresh air – maybe in the countryside, your garden or a park.

2. Focus on a place or spot in the distance and imagine you are filled with blue cyan light. As it exudes from you into the atmosphere, this cool, electromagnetic energy freezes, forms icicles on the trees and on the cobwebs, and the light breeze transforms into a fierce frozen wind. Your brilliant thoughts and ideas spill into the spirit of the landscape.

3. Imagine these thoughts circling the world, giving out the liquid diamond of your mind – those gems crystallising in the material world and the great minds of our civilisation, yet always connected to the universal nature of Uranian thought.

4. Feel blessed with this clear-cut mind, and whenever you are in need of inspiration, think about how your ruling planet, Uranus, is not only an ice giant, but also a diamond in the sky.

GLAMOUR FUN

For all their progressive thinking, Aquarians are also quite ambitious in the corridors of glamour and power. They like to mingle with the jet-set, politicians, celebrities and academics. It's quite smart, really, as that's where they can upset the status quo with their madcap ideas or unique trends of thought.

If you're thinking, 'Well, no – that's not me', think a little deeper. As much as you may be one of those Aquarians who's more up for a spot of backpacking or running a tattoo shop, isn't there something rather glamorous about imagining yourself on the steps of the Taj Mahal or even the White House?

Try this simple ritual to understand how glamour makes you feel good to be you.

1. Dress up in a wacky but glamorous outfit you adore, or maybe one that you improvise in the moment. Be as charismatic or as shocking as you like and step out into the world. But regardless of whether or not you shock a few people, what is more important is how it makes *you* feel.

Glamour is a magical enchantment that exudes from the Aquarius aura and, once expressed, bestows on you a sense of self-empowerment. So enjoy being as daring, avant-garde or outrageous as you like.

FACE VISUALISATION

Do you really know yourself? Practise this fun face test to find out if what you see in your mind equates to what you see in the mirror – which is, of course, an illusion of who you really are. As an Aquarian, you are pretty sure you know who you are, but when you actually have to express your thoughts through artistic practice, you might find you surprise even yourself!

You will need:

* A pen/pencil/paints
* Paper

1. Sit comfortably, find a sense of stillness, close your eyes and imagine your face. What features stand out for you? What do you like about your face, and what don't you like?

2. Once you have visualised a vivid portrait of yourself in your mind, open your eyes and try to reproduce this image on paper. It doesn't matter if it's in proportion, a cartoon, a mess of colour or lines without meaning;

it can be anything – just keep creating a self-portrait from what is in your mind.

3. When you have finished, find a mirror or a photo of yourself. See if there's any resemblance between what you have drawn and what you see in the mirror or photograph. Observe how you imagined some things about yourself that perhaps aren't there? Or is the mirror lying? Is the photo a true likeness of you, or is that an illusion, too?

4. Either way, you have now put your mind to the task of identifying who you, as a radical, freedom-loving Aquarius, actually are. Taking steps to acknowledge your features, your image and your self-portrait is one of the best ways to start practising Aquarian self-understanding.

GOING SOLO

Aquarius, out of all the sun signs (apart, perhaps, from Aries and Sagittarius) prefers an independent pathway in life. There are times when you choose solitude over friendship and loving partners. But in that solitude, you discover much about yourself. So repeat this mantra every day; learn it, write it in your journal, on sticky notes on your fridge, on your mirror – anywhere you may glance or look – and admire and nurture the autonomous person you are:

'I follow the pathway less travelled by many, for it leads to knowing more of myself.'

BE NICE TO YOURSELF

When was the last time you bought yourself flowers? It may be that you do it on a regular basis, but this time do so with care and attention for the flowers themselves, the pot you place them in, their position in your home. Be aware of how a flower grows: the way it evolves from bud to blossom, and then how it withers and how you dispose of it – in an environmentally friendly way, wishing it well.

Give gratitude to the flowers for brightening your day, for their presence in your life, and be aware of how nice you were to give them to yourself.

Practise the art of being nice to yourself and respecting the little gifts you can give from and to the world around you – then you can care about the world, too.

MAGIC POUCH FOR CREATIVE INSPIRATION

We all have an inner witch inside us, but depending on our sun sign, our witchy qualities will manifest in various ways, and we can work more successfully with some forms of magic than others. The Aquarian witch is innovative and finds ways to perform magic spells in subtle or ingenious ways. When you are in need of inspiration or you want to help to inspire others, try the following charm to remind you of your bewitching talent.

You will need:
* A small white pouch or muslin cloth
* A pen with waterproof ink
* Sandalwood essential oil
* A handful of lavender flowers (fresh or dried)
* A red ribbon

1. On a new crescent-moon evening, take your pouch or piece of cloth and mark it with the symbol for Aquarius with waterproof ink.

2. Drizzle a few drops of sandalwood oil on to the lavender flowers and place them in the pouch.

3. Tie the pouch or cloth up with the red ribbon.

4. Keep the pouch with you until the full moon to transform great ideas into realistic schemes and to enhance your creative flow. You can also carry it with you to inspire other people with your future plans.

MAKING A GOOD IMPRESSION

Although on the outside Aquarians appear not to care too much what other people think about them, they secretly do. In fact, if they are not causing some sort of reaction in a partner, friend, colleague or onlooker, they will do their utmost – whether consciously or not – to provoke one, be it positive or negative.

The exercise below will reveal how others' opinions of your Uranian personality do matter, and how you can use this to your advantage.

You will need:

* A mirror
* Pen and paper

1. Sit before the mirror.

2. Write down a list of ten of your positive attributes.

3. Draw an image of yourself with labels, such as 'kind', 'easy-going', 'friendly' and so on.

4. Next, write down a list of ten qualities *you think* that other people might see in you, such as 'cool', 'quirky' and so on. Now draw an image of how you imagine this other 'you' to be.

5. Compare the two images and the lists. Ask yourself: do you need to change anything about yourself, or is the image *you think* others have of you great, better or more realistic than the one you have of yourself? Do you need to change anything about yourself before you can change the world?

Asking yourself these sorts of questions will enable you to understand how to make the kind of impression that you, as an Aquarian, want to make on other people. Their opinion of you matters if you want to get anywhere in the world.

....

A LETTER TO THE UNIVERSE

Uranus is one of the so-called 'outer planets', in that it is concerned with what the eminent psychologist Carl Jung called 'the collective unconscious' – in other words, the archetypal and mysterious nature of life that flows through all humanity. The Aquarian mind has a talent for tapping into this collective unconscious (also known as the universal energy flow) where, according to Jung, all innovation, invention and ideas originate. To connect more closely to this numinous place and find a wealth of original ideas to promote your care for the planet, practise the following ritual every new crescent moon.

You will need:

* A white candle
* A clear quartz crystal
* A pen and paper
* An envelope

1. Light the candle and place the crystal in front of it.

2. Focus into the depths of the crystal, scanning for any plays of light from the candle flame, any shadows, images or shapes that appear.

3. Write down on your paper anything that you see in the crystal, no matter what. You don't have to write precise details; just let your mind wander and flicker like the flame, and inspiration will come to you. This random list, however disjointed, odd or erratic, is your letter to the Universe.

4. Place your letter in the envelope.

5. Seal your intention for greater cosmic inspiration by dropping a little candle wax on to the envelope (tilting it ever so gently for a few seconds).

6. Blow out the candle, fold the paper and thank the Universe for your connection.

7. Place the letter under your pillow and soon you will be sparkling with genius ideas.

....

GIVING

In our relationship with the 'world out there', we give, receive, go up, down, move towards and away. Equally, we must balance the desire for any kind of success with being grateful – not only for what we may receive, but also in appreciation of other people's success.

1. Resolve that every time you think of someone, you think 'good' things about them. The Aquarian mind may well struggle against this to begin with and say, 'Hang on, I'm not sure how much I like the boss ...' However, the more you think kind thoughts about people, the more you will be putting out positive energy to shape your own destiny.

2. Try to practise the art of giving at least once a day, by literally giving someone a smile, a compliment, a friendly email, praise or genuine sympathy.

3. Receive Nature's offerings readily, too – if it's raining, be glad for it; if there's a drought, know that there is meaning behind it: a drought could be ruining livelihoods, but it also presents a creative opportunity to act and save lives in the future. Use this mindset for any problem you encounter.

This practice will help to send out your quirky Aquarian thoughts and ideas, which can only come back around to benefit you in the future.

SUCCESS STORY

There is an ancient Greek myth that particularly resonates with the Aquarian quest and maximising your personal success story.

Pandora (meaning either all-gifted or all-giving) was the first mortal woman on Earth. Her partner, Prometheus (the giver of fire to humanity), owned a jar (which has since, erroneously, become known as a box) in which all the blessings and curses of mankind had been placed by the gods. According to some scholars, curiosity overcame Pandora, and as she opened the jar all the contents, both good and evil, spilled out into the world, apart from 'hope', which was saved. Optimistic scholars believe hope was saved as a treasure for humanity's later use. More pessimistic writers believe hope was imprisoned in the jar, and thus mankind has no hope, only sin. Here, you are going to create your own jar of qualities, using the positive outcome of this myth as a symbol for the power of storing secrets and guarding treasure.

You will need:

* A jar you like – preferably one with a lid to 'contain' the contents
* Some stones or pebbles, or scraps of paper
* A pen or pencils

1. Make a list of both negative and good qualities. Perhaps choose from:

Anger

Pride

Hate

Fear

Love

Wonder

Compassion

Gratitude

Harmony

Peace

Belief

Care . . . and so on

2. Write or draw one quality on each stone or scrap of paper.

3. Place the stones or scraps in the jar, close it and keep it somewhere safe.

4. Whenever you're in need of creating a new personal success story, open the jar and take a leap of faith as to what you will draw out. Even if it's something negative, it has value by telling you, perhaps, what needs 'attention' in your life or in the world at large right now.

Sometimes that Aquarian quest for goodness for all can uncover a can of worms, but it also leads to making a radical difference to the world. So don't hesitate – if you see a Pandora's jar that needs opening, take a risk and open it.

....

WHO DWELLS WITHIN?

There is a mesmerising painting by the symbolist artist George Frederic Watts, entitled *Dweller in the Innermost*. The angelic, enigmatic, hazy figure depicted seems spiritual and mystical, but also, in her golden glow, shows human self-acceptance.

How self-aware are you? Can you be a silent observer, without judging, without seeing your feelings as a sign of weakness? Be the dweller in the innermost of you with this simple visualisation:

1. Sit comfortably and find stillness.

2. Imagine you are an angel, or some great goddess – any image of the divine you like – or even an alien. This spiritual being lives within you, and observes the daily goings on in your mind, and in your psyche.

3. Observe the difference between thinking and feeling. Be conscious of how you like to surprise or shock others and be different, standing out from the crowd. Be aware of how you can blot out emotions, such as sadness, anger, fear and vulnerability. Let the

61

dweller in the innermost observe, not judge, even – just see all of you.

4. Now come out of your visualisation.

In the days to follow, whenever you sense a feeling, reaction or desire arise, let it do so, and observe it as if you are your own innermost dweller; be aware of how it is, and let it be. You don't have to do anything with it. It is not a weakness; it is a new-found Aquarian strength.

Relationships

Freedom-loving Aquarians are broad-minded and believe in unconditional and unconventional love, too. The aloof Water Bearer rarely reaches down into the murky waters of emotion for fear of discovering they have feelings, too. In intimate relationships, Aquarians flounder, however much they appear at ease on the surface. While some signs of the zodiac thrive on long-term commitment, Aquarians believe non-exclusive love is best for them, and this single-minded approach can sometimes leave them, well, single. Everyone to Aquarius is 'a friend', including romantic or long-term interests. Yet long-term relationships work for the Water Bearer when a potential 'partner' is as much of a free bird as they are and accepts there are many other 'friends' who will come and go in Aquarius's world.

The following practices will help you to attract the kind of love that gives you the freedom to be you and ensure that you care truly for your relationship needs.

....

LONGITUDES AND
LATITUDES OF LOVE

Thousands of years ago, the positions of the stars and constellations were used to navigate across land or sea. In fact, the stars also taught us how to find our way in love. The word 'desire' is rooted in the Latin *de sidere*, meaning 'from the stars', as well as in *desiderare*, which means 'await what the stars will bring'. In love, we wonder what the stars will bring and how we can navigate our desires.

Two ancient Greek astronomers, Eratosthenes and, later, Hipparchus proposed imaginary lines around the Earth, which we know as longitude and latitude. These were used to measure, map out, plot the globe instead of the stars. In 'love' there are also latitudes and longitudes, in that we have been given a traditional set of coordinates with which to follow the conventions of romance and marriage.

As an Aquarian, however, you may find the latitudes and longitudes of conventional relationships restrictive and incompatible with your desire for freedom. So honour your own individuality, which reflects your need for unconditional love. You don't have to go down the conventional route – instead, navigate by the stars; in other words, use your intuition, and maybe, with some astrological knowledge, you will be able to follow your desires.

PERFECT HARMONY AND ROMANCE

Of course, there are times when Aquarians do give chase in the world of love, as it's a natural instinct they can't always escape. So here's a way to nurture the seductive side of your nature and enhance romantic success.

In medieval alchemy, gold and silver were symbolic of sun and moon, masculine and feminine, thoughts and feelings. It was believed that the mystical union of these opposites would create not only pure 'gold' but an 'intelligence of the heart' – an Aquarius motif, if ever there was one. Use this ritual to enrich all forms of Uranian relationships, whether for closer friendship, the success of long-distance or unconditional love, commitment to another but with no promises, balancing an independent lifestyle with love, developing agreements and compromise and so much more.

You will need:
* 2 candles: 1 gold and 1 silver
* 2 rings: 1 gold and 1 silver
* 2 ribbons: 1 gold and 1 silver

1. On the evening of a new crescent moon, light the two candles.

2. Place the gold ring in front of the silver candle, and the silver ring in front of the gold candle.

3. Focus on the flames for a few moments, then take up the gold ribbon and loop it through the silver ring, and take up the silver ribbon and loop it through the gold ring.

4. Now knot the two ribbons together at each end, to form one complete loop between the two rings. As you do so, say: 'With gold and silver, I find solar and lunar harmony in my relationships'.

5. Keep the rings and ribbons under your pillow for one lunar cycle to work the power of heartfelt connection between you and others.

FINDING THE RIGHT ONE

Aquarian eccentric or not, you're only human, and there will be times when you yearn for the loving arms of another, or just to have a pal to accompany you on your personal journey. Here's a simple charm to attract the right kind of love into your life.

You will need:

* A pen and paper
* A piece of amber (or amber jewellery)
* 4 pieces of rose quartz

1. Write in the centre of the paper a list of qualities you seek in a potential partner.

2. Draw a large circle around the list to seal your intention.

3. Place the amber in the centre of the circle and the four rose-quartz pieces outside it to mark the compass points at east, west, south and north, connecting you to the power of the Universe.

4. Simply say, 'Bring to me the one who is written here below, so that we can share and enjoy love for one another'.

5. Fold the paper and store it somewhere safe with the rose-quartz crystals. Take the amber with you wherever you go, to attract the right kind of partner.

PART TWO

Caring For Your Body

In the midst of winter, I finally learned that there was in me an invincible summer.

Albert Camus, *Actuelles*

Here, you will discover alternative ways to look after and nurture your body, not just as a physical presence, but its connection to mind and spirit, too. This section gives you a wide range of ideas, from using sun-sign crystals to protect your physical and psychic self to fitness, diet and beauty tips. There are specific chakra practices and yoga poses especially suited to your sun sign, not forgetting bath-time rituals and calming practices to destress and nurture holistic wellbeing.

The Aquarian pathway to physical wellbeing is pretty much, well, your way. However, a simple routine to get you energised for the day could consist of – in any order you like – a morning stretch, a healthy breakfast, a shower, a walk in the fresh air and a cup of green tea. This would probably be enough to remind you about physical self-care, and could be enough to read before you close this book. But hang on . . .

Traditionally, Aquarius is associated with the ankles, lower legs and peripheral circulatory system. You're also wired into the electromagnetic fields of your aura (see Glossary, p. 117), chakra system (see pp. 20 and 91) and the interchange with the various energy fields in the cosmos. As you are acutely sensitive to these invisible frequencies, energy-based therapies such as acupuncture, reiki or chakra healing will appeal to you. With your enthusiasm for all things technological, you can overexpose yourself to negative geopathic stress (various electromagnetic and invisible energies found in the environment), so balance this with crystal healing and protection.

To get you started, here's a selection of body rituals and practices you can try out to keep your body in shape and in harmony with your inspirational mind.

Fitness And Movement

Exercise such as Pilates, hatha yoga or just a long, bracing walk are all ways in which Aquarians can avoid the kind of organised routines that leave them feeling ice cold as Uranus. Or, if you feel like trying something new, just for the sake of it, how about the wacky Brazilian martial-art *capoeira* exercises or the Tibetan Seamm-Jasani holistic method – a cross between yoga and tai chi? These disciplines combine both breathing and movement for vitality and inner energy.

Air signs also need fresh air. Getting outside and into Nature gives you both the opportunity to work out your body with some aerobic exercise and the time to reflect and be inspired with great thoughts for the good of the planet.

....

MORNING STRETCH

A morning stretch brings balance to mind and body – it's a great way to start the day to bring positivity and a sense of purpose, or before you dive into your ocean of humanitarian good work:

1. Lie flat on your back on the floor, on a yoga mat or carpet.

2. Reach your arms up towards the sky first, then stretch each one in turn, trying to reach higher and higher.

3. Lower your arms back down to the floor above your head and stretch each one in turn, as if making them longer.

4. Now do the same with your legs. First, point one up towards the sky, then the other, then lower them to the floor, stretching them out, as if to elongate them.

5. Finally, stretch your arms and legs at the same time, until you have stretched yourself out so much that you feel as if you have grown several inches. Stay in the stretch for one more in- and out-breath, then return to your normal size.

Once you've done this stretch, you'll feel looser, relaxed and free of all tension.

EMPOWERING YOGA POSE

Enhancing life-force energy, strengthening and toning the body and promoting good circulation in the ankles and calves, yoga is, of course, made for you. With the well-known 'downward facing dog' pose, you will see the world from a different perspective as you look down and behind you:

1. From the table-top position (hands and knees on the floor, wrists beneath your shoulders, knees below hips), curl your toes and push up and back, straightening your legs.

2. Lift your tail bone high, towards the sky and, at the same time, push your heels to the floor, or as near as you can get them.

3. Let your shoulder blades relax and your head hang down between your shoulders and arms, so you can see your legs.

4. Hold this pose for 1 minute, as you gaze at the world from an upside-down point of view.

Try this pose and see how it can give you an empowering flash of brilliant thinking. It may even inspire you with an innovative way to reform humanity.

A HOP, A SKIP AND A JUMP

As you don't want to be like everyone else, why not get out into the wide-open countryside and enjoy a revitalising hop, skip and jump in Nature? With the practice below, you can incorporate body movement with aerobic exercise, boost metabolism and promote greater flexibility and tone for those Aquarius hot-spots – the ankles and lower legs.

1. Take a good, brisk walk and find a place where you can hop, skip and jump forwards on a grassy surface.

2. Before you start hopping, look to the sky, connect to the Universe, and say, 'I hop, I skip, I jump to improve all mobility and balance my physique'.

3. Then take one big hop, followed by one big skip and finally one long jump.

4. Repeat twice more, and then stand quietly for a few moments, enjoying the sense of vitalised energy you feel in your legs and ankles.

This simple practice will give any hike or walk in the country a madcap Aquarian edge.

Nutrition

Although, as an Aquarian, you'd rather be out saving the world than worrying about what's in your fridge, there are times when you obsess about the kinds of food you're eating, and whether they're doing any good or harm to the planet.

You've likely already opted for organic food, and if there's any new fad, you've probably already tried (if not invented) it. Because you are sensitive to the ecosystem and electromagnetic energies, the benefits of eating raw or slightly cooked vegetables and plants will align you to the planet's unique energy system. Don't forget to include foods such as nuts, pulses, root vegetables and whole grains to remind you of the gifts of the Earth itself.

A WEEKEND DETOX

What stresses you out (apart from the state of the world) is listening to all the health 'experts' and the theories you already know. The stresses of daily living can build toxins in the body, so to redress the balance a good spring clean of your system is needed now and again, and the best time for this is during a waning moon, when your body can release toxins more easily.

* Plan a raw-food or juice diet for a couple of days.
* Drink at least 4 pints of spring water over the course of each day.

This body declutter will act as a great cleansing device, revitalising your body and spirit.

SPICE IT UP

That Aquarian spirit of adventure in the great outdoors can be enjoyed better with a spicy, uplifting drink (especially in cold weather).

You will need:
* 1 or 2 cups of water (depending on how much you think you'll drink)
* 2 teaspoons of instant coffee, or to taste (decaf if you prefer)
* 1 whole clove
* ½ cinnamon stick
* grated nutmeg
* Sugar, to taste (optional)

1. Put everything into a small pan.

2. Bring to the boil, then remove from the heat, cover and leave to infuse for 5 minutes.

3. Strain and discard the spices. Stir in sugar, if required, reheat quickly, then pour into your Thermos flask.

This simple mulled coffee will empower you with vitalising energy. Whether you're out on a hike or off on a bike, take it with you for a warming, zingy coffee experience.

Beauty

You know what makes you feel good to be you, and you also know you like to shock, dumbfound and unnerve others, standing out from the crowd you're so keen to transform. So if you fancy wearing yellow lipstick one day, pampering your skin with mashed avocados the next or simply using soap and water another, then that's the pure delight of being Aquarius. And in doing so, the likelihood is that you'll discover some amazing new product for wrinkle-free skin and we'll all be most grateful! Even though you may not be a fashion guru or beauty expert, you could become one as you intuitively know what people need. Use this gift of tapping into the collective unconscious to benefit yourself, too.

MASSAGE PARLOUR

In a perfect world, you'd love a back massage every day, but there are so many more important things for you to worry about – like keeping fossil fuels in the ground, protecting forests, discovering a breakthrough in technology – that your body does sometimes come last. But at least once in a lunar cycle (preferably during a waning or dark-of-the-moon phase, when you can release, let go and generally destress from the worries of the world) delight and treat yourself to a massage.

Obviously, you'll need someone else to do this for you; a friend or partner would be preferable to a professional massage therapist, simply because you could have more 'fun', if so inclined. A friendly massage may also encourage you to be more interested in reviving your sense of touch, a magical and comforting energy, which connects you to the universal life-force.

Here's a simple back-massage technique you can get your pal or partner to do:

1. Lie on your front.

2. Get your partner to gently stroke your back with both hands, perhaps alternating them or simultaneously, as if they were stroking a cat. If you want to use massage oil, then do so, but it isn't essential.

3. After about two or three minutes of all-over stroking, they should begin the kneading technique, pressing firmly with fingers or even knuckles into muscles and flesh, as if kneading dough. This is particularly beneficial for shoulder muscles and will release all your worldly tensions.

4. Finally, ask them to restore energy levels with a percussive movement – perhaps lightly and quickly striking alternate sides of their hands to all areas of your back.

When your massage is finished, enjoy some tea together – or whatever takes your fancy –and feel relaxed and chilled.

REJUVENATING BATH TIME

Here's a bathing ritual to restore and rejuvenate brain cells and physicality, so you're ready for a new wave of Uranian trailblazing ideas.

You will need:
* 4 white tea lights
* Epsom salts (or any other bath salts you prefer)
* 4 pieces of lapis lazuli
* A piece of red carnelian
* Frankincense essential oil

1. Light the candles and place one at each corner of your bath.

2. Run the water, adding the salts.

3. Place the four lapis lazuli pieces beside the candles, and the red carnelian stone at the far end of the bath opposite your head end.

4. Drizzle a few drops of frankincense oil into the bath.

5. As you sink into the water, focus on the red carnelian stone for a few minutes and relax in the bath for as long as you desire.

6. Keep the crystals in a safe pouch to reuse for this bath ritual whenever required. Within a day or so, you will be filled with exciting, inspirational thoughts.

CHAKRA BALANCE

The body's chakras are the epicentres of the life-force energy flowing through all things (see p. 20). As the traditional ruler of Aquarius is Saturn, the associated chakra is the root or base chakra (located at the base of the spine). This energy centre keeps you in touch with the planet and its 'roots', the base of all that we are as physical entities.

The base chakra provides a sense of wholeness and security; its energy controls the basic functioning needs of the body. When your base chakra is underactive, you feel threatened by those who seem more determined to succeed than you; you would be unable to get any project under way or finished and loath to take responsibility for your actions. If this chakra is overactive, however, you may become too self-opinionated – totally fixated on your own belief and not listening to anyone else. You might even advise others to do things you wouldn't dream of doing yourself.

To subdue an overactive base chakra, carry or wear aquamarine, the crystal of calm, serenity and poise; for an underactive base chakra, reinforce and rebalance by wearing or carrying obsidian, a crystal associated with empowerment, stability and self-confidence.

General Wellbeing

It's nice to have a feeling that all's well with the world, and we are surrounded by goodness and giving it out, too. The following practices will enable you to balance your own physical presence with that of the environment, bringing harmony and ensuring that your Aquarian sense of wellbeing is a delightful cosmic experience.

UNDER THE STARS

As an Aquarian, your sleep patterns are pretty much all over the place, so take advantage of your ability to stay awake late or rise early, and plan to sleep out under the stars on a fine, clear night with a friend.

Whether you opt for a sleeping bag or a sun lounger in the garden, try to experience the night in all its glory. And if sleeping outside is not an option for you, maybe move your bed beneath your window, tie back the curtains and turn off all lights. If you're lucky enough to have a clear night, with its amazing tapestry of stars, no light pollution from cities or streetlamps and the sounds and smells of flowers, nocturnal animals and even a few falling stars, you will be blessed with cosmic wellbeing. If you see a falling star, wish upon it, and indulge in the vista of the Universe beyond and within you.

Sleeping under the stars will make you feel you are part of the Universe itself, and experience the feeling of being a true cosmic caretaker.

TIME OUT IN NATURE

Banish your computer and mobile phone and enjoy some time out in Nature. Just be sure to let people know where you are going and for how long, so they don't worry.

Here are some ways to enjoy your time out:

* Walk barefoot on a beach, the grass, in the meadow, through wild flowers.
* Explore unknown paths of a wood or forest, and discover the hidden beauty of lichen, tree trunks or fallen leaves, wild flowers or weeds.
* Go for a long cross-country hike or use a bike.
* Just sit in your garden, if you have one, or a green space or park, and watch the world go by – that is the birds and the insects at work.
* Plant a tree or bush in a wild place (if you have the right) or in your garden.
* Sit on a windy hill and enjoy the rain if it falls; appreciate and give thanks for being part of the physical world.

* Appreciate and admire the view or the landscape of somewhere you know really well but have never stopped to observe before. Connecting with a place you usually take for granted will give you a renewed perspective on the world.
* Sit and listen to the birds or the rustle of trees in the wind. Anything you hear in Nature is, in a way, Nature's way of communicating to you. There may be hidden messages that only you can interpret, so why not have a go? As Aquarians love to learn any unusual language, this is one you are sure to master, and it will nurture your mind.

Any of these activities will do wonders to restore your natural energy balance and may inspire you to do things that benefit Nature, too. Give thanks for being able to appreciate what is around you, and for having a presence here on planet Earth.

CRYSTAL PROTECTION

The protective energy from various crystals safeguards your environment from negative electromagnetic or psychic energy. Here's a crystal grid (crystals laid out in a specific symbolic pattern) to bring security and harmony to the spaces in your home. This grid incorporates the crystals geared to enhance and boost your Aquarian qualities of self-reliance and optimism and protect you from negativity.

You will need:
* A piece of amber (for self-reliance)
* 2 pieces of citrine (for creative thought)
* 2 pieces of smoky quartz (for grounding)
* 4 pieces of black tourmaline (for general protection)

Before you place the grid, thank the stones for protection and happiness in the home and handle them with the same respect and kindness as if they were your friends.

1. Find a place in the west corner of your home where you can leave the grid safely – perhaps a designated sacred space or just a windowsill.

2. Place the piece of amber to mark the centre point.

3. Place the pieces of citrine to the north and south of the amber and the smoky quartz to the east and west, all a few inches apart.

4. Place the four black tourmaline pieces to form the four corners of a square, so that they form an X between the other four points.

5. Lastly, blow on each crystal (one breath per crystal – so nine breaths in total) to instil them with your own energy.

The crystals are now programmed to absorb all negativity and to nourish you with harmonious protection.

PART THREE

Caring For Your Soul

The most beautiful emotion we can experience is the mystical. It is the power of all true art and science.

Albert Einstein

This final section offers you tailored, fun, easy and amazing ways to connect to and care for your sacred self. This, in turn, means you will begin to feel at one with the joyous energy of the Universe. You don't have to sign up to any religion or belief system (unless you want to) – just take some time to experience uplifting moments through your interaction with the spiritual aspects of the cosmos. Care for your sun sign's soul centre, and you care about the Universe, too.

Aquarians might live in beach huts, wish on falling stars and wear silly hats, but they are often quite sceptical about anything with that flaky label, 'spiritual'. Intellectually, they're well informed about esoteric beliefs and ideologies and probably ahead of their time, and they often develop an abstract concept of what the soul, spirit or divine are all about. But how in touch are you with your sacred self?

According to most pagan and neopagan spiritualities, the divine can be experienced within ourselves, through our interactions with the world, Nature and the Universe. But this means we have to care enough about it in the first place to try it out.

By caring about your soul or spirit, you are caring

for the universal energy that permeates all. Like many Uranian-ruled people, you might swim with dolphins, visit a retreat centre, chill out in a spa and just 'be' or travel to sacred places, stand in awe of a great mountain or just get off the beaten track and be at one with Nature – all these experiences will bring you an awareness of the spirituality within yourself. And here are some other ideas to get you started.

URANUS BRINGS ME THE LIFE THAT I CHOOSE

When we know what really matters to us in life and what gives us a sense of purpose – sometimes called our 'vocation' or 'calling' – we feel a closer connection to our own sacred solar light within. To enhance this Aquarian sense of calling and to expand your awareness of what truly matters to you, try this simple Uranian ritual on a full-moon evening.

You will need:
* An image of the planet Uranus (a photo, painting or other)
* A tea light
* An image of yourself (photo, self-portrait or something that represents you)
* A pen and paper

1. Put the Uranus image on a table.

2. Light the candle and focus on the picture for a moment to relax and find stillness.

3. Place the image of yourself on top of the planet's image to connect you symbolically to Aquarius's ruler's power.

4. Now write the following on the paper and place it on top of your picture:

I am connected to my sun and the planet Uranus.
I am connected to the moon's cycles.
I am connected to the calling of All.
I am a child of the Universe now.
As the world turns once more, I will know my Truth.

Leave the papers together until next full moon, and you will feel a deeper connection to your Uranian soul; you may even hear 'the calling' and know which unusual or inspiring Aquarian direction to take on the next stage of your life journey.

SOLAR MAGIC

Even if you can't sit and watch the summer solstice, at least take time to watch a sunrise and a sunset, preferably on the same day, to give yourself a sense of time and movement, the rhythm and power of the sun's cycle. Aquarians like to experiment, re-form or recycle ideas and experiences, but the one you can't change (yet) is at the very core of your existence: the sun's daily motion.

You may have to check the weather forecast, to ensure that you'll get some sighting of the sun – if it's very cloudy or foggy, perhaps put it off for another day? Then plan your timing, so that you are in a place where the sun rises above hills or the sea (to make it more spectacular) and then, later on, in another place where it sets or drops dramatically beneath the horizon. It might be worth remembering that the sun is a dying star, so respect its current life-giving rays wherever and whenever you can.

After you have experienced the magic of the sun, your Aquarian mind and spirit will be inspired to discover new approaches to all astral phenomena, and the Universe – within and without you – becomes a much more exciting place.

YOUR RAINFOREST

This visualisation will connect you to the sacredness of the planet and help you to realise that you are part of it. Understanding your own Uranian desire to nurture the world means you're also caring for your spiritual self.

Visualise inside yourself a rainforest – a place of beauty, humidity; silent, dripping with raindrops after the monsoon.

In this dense jungle or tropical forest, there is such a diversity of life that you will be surprised by what you find there. Imagine beasts, insects, bugs, beauty, hidden flowers and magical plants.

Your thoughts, feelings and your soul are also found in this beautiful landscape. Protect this rainforest of yours as you would those of the natural world. It is a place to shelter in for a while and to watch the sacred centre of yourself evolve, grow, await the rains and be nourished by them.

When you come out of your visualisation, you will begin to understand the depths and joys that are hidden within you. And maybe you'll take that Aquarian bus ride to save other real-life rainforests, too?

FLASH OF INSIGHT

To improve your connection to the gift of intuition and those sudden flashes of insight Aquarians often experience, perform this little ritual whenever you become aware of imminent stormy weather or thunder and lightning in the distance.

You will need:
* A pouch
* A handful of (say, 5) small polished or natural stones
* A red ribbon
* A clear quartz crystal

Note: remain inside your home for this ritual; never venture out during violent or stormy weather.

1. As the storm approaches, place the pouch, stones and crystal on a table, and say the following:

'When lightning strikes so does my mind
With flashes bold and thunder signs
This spell will bring me insights true
To know the truth and see the view.

2. Now place the five stones in the pouch, one by one, and repeat the spell each time.

3. Seal your intention by tying the red ribbon around your pouch, then hold the quartz crystal in your hand and say, 'Thank you Universe for blessing me with the power of wisdom in the lightning world'.

4. If the storm arrives before you finish the ritual, don't be concerned. In fact, you may feel humbled and empowered by its presence, or that its power is bringing you enlightened thinking. Hold the crystal until the storm has passed, and in the days to come you will be ready to act upon any flashes of insight.

THE LANGUAGE OF THE UNIVERSE

Does the Universe speak? Well, you probably get those odd moments when you put scepticism aside and attempt to work out what those hunches, intuitive moments and so on really mean. The language of symbols can help you to develop and care for your intuitive powers rather than dismiss them.

You will need:
* A pen and paper
* A piece of citrine
* A large reference book (dictionary, encyclopaedia or similar)

1. Write your name on the piece of paper and place the citrine above your name.

2. Open your chosen book totally at random, maybe flicking through the pages with your eyes closed, until something inside you says, 'Stop'.

3. Without looking, run your finger across the open pages and, again, when you feel the moment is right, still your finger and open your eyes.

4. Look at the nearest word or short phrase and write it down on the paper above the crystal.

Use this divination technique to connect to the message the Universe is sending you. Whichever words you pluck out of the book are about you, right now, this moment. Each word is simply a 'symbol' (the word is rooted in an ancient Greek word meaning, 'that which is thrown together') with which you are going to experiment (a Uranian pleasure trip) during the day. See if you can relate any experiences or encounters to this word as the day goes on. If you still can't relate, try again another day, until you start to understand the language.

Once you realise that a random word chosen in a moment of time (which may, in fact, have chosen you) has meaning, as does anything symbolic that happens during the day, you will also begin to open up to the messages sent to you via your intuition, another way in which the Universe communicates what you need to know.

....

FOLLOW YOUR DREAM . . .

In Greek mythology, Prometheus (meaning forethought) stole fire from the gods and gave it to mankind. In revenge, Zeus chained him to a rock where an eagle devoured his liver every day. Each night, the liver grew back again, endlessly repeating this torment. (By the way, the ancient Greeks believed the liver was the 'seat' of human emotion.) Prometheus was eventually saved from his eternal curse when Heracles killed the eagle.

The Promethean spirit is often likened to the Aquarian drive for progress and beneficial change for all of humanity. So whatever progress, change or invention mean to you – whether they're all about the little things you give to your friends (advice, understanding, compassion, a cup of tea) or something grander (perhaps changing the way humanity thinks, or setting up a pop-up shop on Mars) – embrace forethought and connect to the sacred solar light and fire of your inner Prometheus with the simple affirmation below. Wherever you are – driving the car, in a crowded place, alone in the country or just whenever you feel that soulful sense of universal oneness rise within you, say:

'Like Prometheus I give the solar fire of myself to All, but the eagle cannot harm me, for I am blessed with an Aquarian soul that is forever reinventing the future.'

This ritual will help you to follow your current Aquarian dream (or whatever your goal is right now), as well as discover your solar purpose.

Last Words

US-born Thomas Edison, the great Aquarian inventor, businessman and pioneer of electricity, said, 'The value of an idea lies in the using of it'. This notion is, of course, at the heart of your Aquarian personality, where innovative ideas inspire you to change the status quo, fuel your visions for improving the world or deliver something life-changing for humanity.

Honour and respect your rebellious individuality, give life to your dreams and nurture your radical humour, your free spirit, your love of the world and all that's in it. Caring for all the qualities of your sun-sign 'selfie' – that amazing depiction of the moment you were born up there in the heavens – means others will love and respect you for who you are. Create your own niche market in the world at large, as a unique statement of your Aquarian dream.

When you care for the zany, unpredictable sunlight of yourself, you care for the world and the Universe, too. By taking time to look after you, you will discover the true happiness you seek, along with the unparalleled joy of becoming who you are.

Resources

Main sites for crystals, stones, candles, smudging sticks, incense, pouches, essential oils and everything needed for the holistic self-care practices included in this book:

holisticshop.co.uk
thepsychictree.co.uk
thesoulangels.co.uk
earthcrystals.com
livrocks.com
artisanaromatics.com

For a substantial range of books (and metaphysical items) on astrology, divination, runes, palmistry, tarot and holistic health, etc.:

thelondonastrologyshop.com
watkinsbooks.com
mysteries.co.uk
barnesandnoble.com
innertraditions.com

For more information on astrology, personal horoscopes and birth-chart calculations:
astro-charts.com (simplest, very user friendly)

horoscopes.astro-seek.com (straightforward)
astrolibrary.org/free-birth-chart (easy to use, with lots of extra information)

Glossary

Aura An invisible electromagnetic energy field that emanates from and surrounds all living beings

Auric power The dominant colour of the aura, which reveals your current mood or state

Chakra Sanskrit for 'wheel', in Eastern spiritual traditions the seven chakras are the main epicentres – or wheels – of invisible energy throughout the body

Dark of the moon This is when the moon is invisible to us, due to its proximity to the sun; it is a time for reflection, solitude and a deeper awareness of oneself

Divination Gaining insight into the past, present and future using symbolic or esoteric means

Double-terminator crystal A quartz crystal with a

point at each end, allowing its energy to flow both
ways

Full moon The sun is at its maximum opposition to
the moon, thus casting light across all of the moon's
orb; in esoteric terms, it is a time for culmination,
finalising deals, committing to love and so on

Geopathic stress Negative energy emanating from
and on the Earth, such as underground water
courses, tunnels, overhead electrical cables and
geological faults

Grid A specific pattern or layout of items
symbolising specific intentions or desires

Horoscope An astrological chart or diagram showing
the position of the sun, moon and planets at the
time of any given event, such as the moment of
somebody's birth, a marriage or the creation of an
enterprise; it is used to interpret the characteristics
or to forecast the future of that person or event

New crescent moon A fine sliver of crescent light
that appears curving outwards to the right in the
northern hemisphere and to the left in the southern
hemisphere; this phase is for beginning new projects,
new romance, ideas and so on

Psychic energy One's intuition, sixth sense or instincts, as well as the divine, numinous or magical power that flows through everything

Shadow side In astrology, your shadow side describes those aspects of your personality associated with your opposite sign and of which you are not usually aware

Smudging Clearing negative energy from the home with a smouldering bunch of dried herbs, such as sage

Solar return salutation A way to give thanks and welcome the sun's return to your zodiac sign once a year (your birthday month)

Sun in opposition The sun as it moves through the opposite sign to your own sun sign

Sun sign The zodiac sign through which the sun was moving at the exact moment of your birth

Waning moon The phase of the moon after it is full, when it begins to lose its luminosity – the waning moon is illuminated on its left side in the northern hemisphere, and on its right side in the southern hemisphere; this is a time for letting go, acceptance and preparing to start again

Waxing moon The phase between a new and a full moon, when it grows in luminosity – the waxing moon is illuminated on its right side in the northern hemisphere and on its left side in the southern hemisphere; this is a time for putting ideas and desires into practice

Zodiac The band of sky divided into twelve segments (known as the astrological signs), along which the paths of the sun, the moon and the planets appear to move

About the Author

After studying at the Faculty of Astrological Studies in London, the UK, Sarah gained the Diploma in Psychological Astrology – an in-depth 3-year professional training programme cross-fertilised by the fields of astrology and depth, humanistic and transpersonal psychology. She has worked extensively in the media as astrologer for titles such as *Cosmopolitan* magazine (UK), *SHE, Spirit & Destiny* and the *London Evening Standard*, and appeared on UK TV and radio shows, including *Steve Wright in the Afternoon* on BBC Radio 2.

Her mainstream mind-body-spirit books include the international bestsellers, *The Tarot Bible, The Little Book of Practical Magic* and *Secrets of the Universe in 100 Symbols*.

Sarah currently practises and teaches astrology and other esoteric arts in the heart of the countryside.

Acknowledgements

I would first like to thank everyone at Yellow Kite, Hodder & Stoughton and Hachette UK who were part of the process of creating this series of twelve zodiac self-care books. I am especially grateful to Carolyn Thorne for the opportunity to write these guides; Anne Newman for her editorial advice, which kept me 'carefully' on the right track; and Olivia Nightingall who kept me on target for everything else! It is when people come together with their different skills and talents that the best books are made – so I am truly grateful for being part of this team.

See the full Astrology Self-Care series here

9781399704885   9781399704915   9781399704588

9781399704618   9781399704649   9781399704670